The Room Next Door

ANDREW DEE

The Room Next Door

Copyright © Andrew Dee 2018

ISBN 978-1-979793-60-5

First printed in the UK in 2018

Designed and edited by The Book Refinery Ltd
www.thebookrefinery.com

All rights reserved. No part of this publication may be reproduced or stored in a retrieval system. No part of this publication may be transmitted, copied in any form or by any means, phonographic, photographic or electric process, mechanical recording or otherwise without written permission from the author.

The advice given is for guidance, information and for entertainment purposes only.

Readers take full responsibility, being of sound mind, for accepting or not accepting and guidance and/or predictions given. All information given in this publication is for the readers use of their own free will.

'Andrew, I see something in you'
Mystic Ed - 2008

Ed and I first spoke to each other in 2008 as guests of Elizabeth Lee-Crowther on her Spirits Calling show, which featured on the Black Country's The Bridge 102FM radio station. Ed was in the studio with his partner, Brian, aka 'Fluffy', and I was a phone-in guest.

I had never heard of Ed, but it wouldn't take long for me to warm to him, as everybody did.

"*I'm ever so popular,*" he said in his own inimitable way, and he was. If you pop 'Mystic Ed' into any search engine, he will appear, mainly as a celebrity psychic but also for his non-psychic abilities.

It was always carnage when Ed went anywhere because he was so outlandish, colourful and gregarious. Publicly, he never took anything seriously and when he was around the conversation always took a risqué turn.

Shortly after my baptism of fire on the radio, Ed asked if we could speak on the phone. I duly obliged and we chatted for well over an hour. It was as if we had known each other forever and we laughed and laughed.

One thing I was not expecting was for Ed's mother in Spirit to make herself known to me. She literally barged in. Ed was sold and said, "*Andrew, you must come over for coffee.*" You couldn't say no to Ed.

I was shocked to discover we only lived about three miles from each other. I lived in Armitage in the Midlands and Ed lived in a bungalow on the Pye Green Road in Cannock. When I arrived there, I realised I'd been down that road many times before, totally unaware of Ed's house.

"*Welcome to my humble abode,*" he said. It was like being greeted by the Queen. He had the room laid out, where I took a seat with him and Fluffy. It really was like '*An Audience With…*' I was given the royal tour, including Angelica's room (his 19-year-old cat) and the cinematic conservatory at the rear of the house.

The time flew by and before long I had to leave to pick up my wife from work.

Ed was so engaging, but death was something that was never far from his mind, and he spoke about it often. Whilst chatting, he asked if I was afraid of dying. I was honest and said it was something I didn't really think about, as when I do my spiritual work I deal with the higher side of life and not the physical loss associated with passing away.

Ed gave me a huge hug before I left and said, "*I'm not afraid of dying, Andrew, and I tell people not to mourn me when I go.*" When I asked why, he replied, "*Because I will only ever be in the room next door, my friend.*"

I never saw Ed again. I'm very sad to say that he passed away in March 2013, but he is certainly not forgotten.

"Only true self awareness will allow you to gain insight into the knowledge required to guide others. Never be afraid to continue evolving."

Contents

1. CALL TO ARMS 11
2. SPIRIT INSPIRATION 21
3. UNDERSTANDING ENERGY 23
4. ALTERED STATES OF CONSCIOUSNESS 25
   Beta waves 26
   Alpha waves 26
5. DISCOVERING THE SELF THROUGH ALTERED
   STATES OF CONSCIOUSNESS 29
   Trusting the World of Spirit 31
6. HEALTH KICKS AND
   EARTHLY RESPONSIBILITIES 35
   Getting the best out of your mediumship 35
   Your earthly responsibilities 37
7. CREATING YOUR SACRED SPACE AND
   GROUND RULES 39
8. FIRST STAGES 43
   Sensitivity 43
   Before you begin 43
9. READY, STEADY 47
   ...Go! 49
10. MEET THE 'CLAIRS' 51
    1. Clairvoyance (Clear Seeing) 51

2. Clairaudience (Clear Hearing) 51
3. Clairsentience (Clear Sensing) 52
4. Claircognizance (Clear Knowing) 52
5. Clairalience (Clear Smelling) 52
6. Clairgustance (Clear Tasting) 53

11. COLLECTING EVIDENCE 55
   Working through the evidence 56
   Good and bad evidence 60
   Common denominators 64

12. 'HEART WALLS' 65

13. EXPECTATION MANAGEMENT, SPIRIT INTELLIGENCE AND PSYCHIC AMNESIA 69
   Expectation Management 69
   Spirit intelligence 71
   Psychic amnesia 73

14. THE MORAL DILEMMA 75

15. HASTA LA PASTA? 77

CLOSING WORDS 79

About the Author 81

INTRODUCTION

Welcome – and thank you for choosing to purchase this 'go-to guide'. Your spirit is a wonderful thing and it can guide you through some of the most difficult times of your life. There are occasions when the sound of your own spirit becomes drowned in the cacophony of modern life and you long to hear it sing again. This is possible, but the steps you need to take have to be deliberate and part of the very fabric of your life. There will be occasions when you'll want to hear what your loved ones in the spirit world have to say, too. This is something you can do yourself, or you can seek the services of somebody else, namely a medium.

Either way, mediumship is something everybody can do. I have proved this in my teachings and I aim to show you how to do it, too. If you are already developing as a medium then I'll show you how to do it for the benefit of others. I have deliberately tried to keep away from the airy-fairy stuff that people want to peddle and have kept my writing to the basics, so that you can understand mediumship for what it really is.

How many times have you heard musicians performing stripped back lounge sets because they want to get back to their roots and to where it all began before huge productions became the norm? This is where I am coming from. There were occasions at the beginning of my development when I asked mediums HOW they connected to spirits. I asked them to show or tell me their answer and demanded they reveal their process. Many could not tell me and that is where I can now step in.

I have taken everything right back to basics for you, so that you'll know what is happening and how to actually connect to your own spirit and the spirit world, as well as build on what you have already achieved.

I could not have written this guidebook ten years ago, or even two years ago. I was armed with plenty of theory, but I needed to bring you my book from a position of true knowledge. The learning process never stops, but there had to come a point when I started to write. That moment came in June 2017.

My notes, jottings and thoughts prior to this moment and beyond now form what you are reading today. This is a living document and I welcome your thoughts and ideas. Modern times have gifted me the ability to update my guide at any point via the wonder of the internet. Any changes will be instant and subsequent purchases will be amended accordingly.

My guide is not a one stop shop for all things mediumistic. It is exactly what it says it is and it should be used as a rule of thumb to accompany any practical studies you undertake. To gain maximum benefit, please read it from cover to cover and utilise the free online meditation I have provided. The link to it is within the text of the book.

You may be studying within an open circle or development group at a church, or any other seat of learning. There are also many private centres and individuals who offer mediumship training, too.

Wherever your own journey began, you will not remain there forever because other doors will open as you network with like-minded individuals.

My own journey began within the churches, for which I will always be grateful. But, as with any schooling, I naturally decided to branch out and challenge myself as well as my mediumship, and you will, too.

Please remember that if you undertake this journey and want to make something of your mediumship, ensure that the word 'COMMITMENT' is part of your vocabulary (if it isn't already).

Whether you are an Olympic athlete, a brain surgeon, an architect or a truck driver, you need dedication and commitment to ensure success in your chosen field.

Mediumship is no different.

Andrew Dee, 2018

1. CALL TO ARMS

Bang – 3000 miles, done and dusted. We touched down in our Hercules C130K transport aircraft, marking another 'positive landing'. "Go! Go! Go! Everybody off, get your kit and start moving. Head for the door on your left," screamed the aircraft loadmaster.

Luckily my eyes were well adjusted to the dark interior of the cigar tube I'd been flying in for the last 30 minutes, and I could see the shaft of light emanating from a doorway, some 50 yards away.

Welcome to Basra Air Station (BAS). It was 3am local time and I had left home some 20 hours earlier. The base was in total darkness because we were at war, but not if you were to ask the politicians!

Earlier in January 2007, I'd found myself at the home of the Royal Air Force Regiment (affectionately known as The Rock Apes) at RAF Honnington in Suffolk for three weeks' pre-deployment training. From our vehicle, we practised anti-ambush attacks and had lessons on Improvised Explosive Devices (IEDs), and how to detect them. We also spent a lot of time on the rifle range, honing our weapons skills. Normally when we were sent on a course, I couldn't wait until the end of it to get home again, but not this time. I would have quite happily stayed there running around like an idiot, soaking wet and freezing cold in a field, because I knew what came next (yes, I know, I volunteered).

RAF Brize Norton (BZN) was my next port of call, as I waited for the inevitably delayed flight to Al Udeid in Qatar before being transported by Hercules to Basra in Iraq. At that time, BZN was almost solely responsible for mass British troop movements, and BZN was the abbreviation on any baggage labels.

Before leaving the UK, I was given time to say my goodbyes. I drove my wife Charlie and my two sons home to Liverpool to see my family, but there is only so long you can drag out eating dinner and making idle chit chat before uttering the words, "Gotta go." I can truthfully say that this was the first time in about 35 years that I can remember my dad hugging me. I still can't remember the last time he told me he loved me, but that is another story. Mum, of course, was in tears.

The following week, I bade my next goodbye to Charlie and the boys. The real killer was putting the boys to bed and trying to ignore the fact I wouldn't see them wake the next day. When it was finally bedtime for me, too, I dreaded putting the light out. With Charlie clinging to me for dear life throughout the night, I got little sleep before I had to make a move at around 4am. To this day, Charlie says that it was the longest day of her life. She was used to me returning home after eight hours at work, but although she trusted her gut instinct that told her I would be safe, she couldn't help wondering if she would ever see me again.

****

Back in Basra, I was being driven around Basra Air Station (BAS) by a jubilant 'Kirky' Kirkhope. I had arrived, which meant he was going home. He would never tell anybody his real first name; it was a secret that he would take to the grave with him.

The next few days were filled with collecting equipment, including body armour and meeting my new contacts, whom I would be dealing with over the next four months whilst taking over the ropes from Kirky.

First rule of tri-service operations: do not call anybody a contact in front of soldiers. A soldier's idea of a contact is a target to be shot at – not somebody you call and exchange views with.

In no time at all I was well into my stride. The troops were working hard and morale within the team was high, mainly due to the banter initiated by Sgt 'Brum' Homer from Bloxwich (which is not in Birmingham at all). A veteran of six 'tours', his team was enlisted from the Royal Marines, Royal Corp of Transport and the inimitable Pioneer Corp. If you haven't heard a 'Black Country' accent before, it is music to the ears and even thinking about 'Brum' today still makes me smile, especially as I don't live far from Bloxwich.

My 'oppo', Flight Lieutenant Andy 'Schoolboy' Wilson, along with Major Paul Bailey, completed the tri-service team. Paul was a fantastic guy who had been a major in the Yorkshire Regiment longer than I had been in the Air Force, some 22 years at that time.

We worked 10-12 hour days and those days were starting to get very warm. By mid March, temperatures were reaching 45°C/115°F by 11am. That's great weather for lying by a pool, but not for much else.

Duty called. There were engineering plans to coordinate, meetings to arrange with the troop commanders who had come in out of 'the field', building works to be completed and tear downs of redundant sites to organise – amongst everything else that was required. On top of all this, I was also involved with the secret communications that allowed us to converse in the theatre of operations and with the UK, using either IT or phones.

'Schoolboy' Andy and his predecessor were responsible for the logistics of anything that wasn't my bag. Trying to coordinate a constantly fluid situation was a nightmare task for them. As with any job, there will be people who do their best and others who will decide they just need to keep on top of everything until they are replaced. There were some unholy messes to sort out. Luckily for me, being on the pure engineering side meant everything was objective. Here is a task, here is the equipment and here are the men to do it. Finish it by this date (which was always yesterday).

I once saw the much-anticipated arrival of a $5m secret communications Portakabin wiped out in the blink of an eye. 'Schoolboy' Andy's predecessor (his name genuinely escapes me, but let's call him Dave) was responsible for ensuring that it arrived and was delivered to the right area for us to install.

"What's so difficult about that?" I hear you ask.

Well, a shortage of lifting equipment was the first issue. 'Dave' managed to somehow hire a crane from downtown Basra. It was not fit for the road, never mind hoisting $5m into the air. It was only going to end one way. Things are improving in Iraq, but when the locals have to think about their day-to-day survival, good old health and safety is not top of the agenda. This was no more evident than when the crane driver's assistant stood on the hook of the crane in his sandals and, while wiping his nose on his unsavoury 'dish-dash', was raised 30ft into the air so he could attach the hook to a lifting strop we had acquired.

'Dave' was not letting a small thing like this stop him from getting the job done. Unfortunately, the crane driver had a bigger job booked in later that morning and time was of the essence. A dichotomy was slowly forming, mainly because 'Dave' had to use the utmost caution (his career was potentially on the line here) and the crane driver was thinking about feeding his family and squeezing as many jobs in as possible. However, the real issue was that they didn't speak the same language. A lot of faffing about ensued due to confusion over hand signals, directions and who was in charge. I watched with bated breath. Then the inevitable crunch was heard. A lot of shouting and waving of arms took place, and the driver's assistant was nowhere to be found.

The cabin had hit a blast wall (designed to minimize the impact of bombs or other such explosive devices). The driver duly dumped the cabin on the roadside and refused to have anything more to do with us. If in doubt, shout a lot and blame the other guy. Of course, the driver disappeared and 'Dave' was left with a ton of paperwork to complete and a one-way chat with the boss. The useless cabin had to be sent back to the UK, where it had taken four months to arrive from in the first place, and a replacement was ordered – not good. A Plan B had to be devised to see how we could have our comms without the comms cabin.

During the day, the heat took its toll while at night constant rocket attacks by the local insurgents got in the way of my beauty sleep. It was actually somebody's job to come up with some sort of report about where the rockets had landed. These were locally known as splat maps. (At one point, HQ had to crack down on people requesting splat mats as souvenirs to show where the bombs had landed during their tour of duty – the colour printing costs had skyrocketed.)

The attacks were mostly ineffective, as the majority had been launched from a pile of rocks or a mound of earth a few miles away and were set off using timing devices. Quite crude really, but then it only takes one to cause mayhem – and it did. Our base was originally built for around 2000 troops. There were, however, more than 5000 residing and working there. Not quite a refugee camp, but living cheek by jowl brought its challenges.

One particular challenge was the rotation of the Resident Infantry Company (RIC). From the day I joined the RAF, I moved around as an individual. The Army tends to move en masse. Mostly they arrive as one and leave as one. During one particular rotation, the current RIC had to vacate their accommodation to allow for the incoming advance party of the new RIC to start taking over.

It was during this changeover that the local militia had a bit of luck. We all lived in cabins that were covered by huge sunshades. Not the type of sunshades that you see in garden centres, but huge corrugated sheets on top of girders. There was a story floating around that the sunshades doubled as a means of deflecting any rockets that hit the base, but they were never going to stop anything.

When a rocket did hit, it came straight through the sunshades and through the roof of a few cabins before heading onwards and coming to rest deep inside the sandbags that surrounded each building along the street. Yes, you guessed it, the cabins were arranged in 'streets'. Believe me when I say it – if the new RIC's arrival hadn't been delayed, there would have been carnage that night.

Another close call took place one evening whilst I was walking back from work. Minibuses, driven by locally employed civilians – mainly from India and Bangladesh – transported us around the base. They ran a circular route and although there was no timetable as such, they were frequent enough, ran at a steady 20mph, and were always accompanied by a heady concoction of Bangla music and body odour. The evening was particularly pleasant on this occasion, however, so I decided to walk.

Ambling along on my own with my body armour and helmet on, a sudden whirring noise followed by a crack, thump and an explosion saw me diving for the nearest ditch. (There were 3ft drainage ditches either side of the dirt roads and these housed personnel shelters, allowing us to take cover during rocket attacks.) Needless to say, it was actually too late and not worth us jumping into the shelter because the mortar round had already exploded on the road. Somehow most of the shrapnel went in the opposite direction from me, but on another day it could have been a different story. The crazy thing is, somehow you enter an altered state, and as we lay there in the personal shelter at the side of the road, we started telling jokes to each other. Delayed shock, maybe, but what else can you do when you're stuck for two hours waiting for the all-clear siren?

The second attack came when I was emailing home. Welfare communication cabins were dotted around the base, allowing the troops to email or call home once a week for 30 minutes. Nothing had a higher priority than the welfare comms. If the troops could not reach their families back home, morale went down and so did performances. The subject of contact with home is serious enough to have been raised as a concern in the Houses of Parliament. Emailing was a big deal because social media was almost non-existent in 2007. Facebook was not the monster it is today and there was certainly no Twitter, Snapchat or Instagram.

Mobile phone messaging was strictly off-limits due to us not wanting calls or messages to be intercepted and used for a possible attack against us. Needless to say, I was emailing Charlie when I heard a whooshing sound followed by a thump and a crack. The next thing I knew, I was lying underneath tables and chairs (luckily with my helmet and body armour on).

Of course, the gallows humour that is so evident in military life bared all again. One minute you can be present, the next gone. The guy who was on the floor opposite me looked up and said, "I can't believe this, I have just changed my uniform and now I am covered in shit again."

Obviously Army!

I had it easy compared to some but I certainly heard enough. We were attacked 600 times in four months, but it was the troops in downtown Basra that were really on the front line. I would often be asleep in my body armour (my helmet on the floor beside me) when I'd hear a muffled explosion then a Tannoy announcement assembling the Incident Response Team (IRT). The IRT was mainly made up of doctors and nurses who would be taken via helicopter into town and straight to the scene. We always knew how bad it was depending on how quickly they returned to base and the military hospital to treat any casualties. If they were back quick, we knew they had no work to do in town because there were no survivors.

Call it professionalism if you will, but when it hits the fan, you just do your job and if everybody is in one piece the next day then it's a job well done.

There are all sorts of casualties during these situations. I remember having to visit the police station in the centre of Basra to do a site survey for some equipment we were due to install. The Army captain, 'Sid', met me there and gave me a tour of the place. He insisted we didn't stand too long as we were in 'Sniper's Alley'. I remember him telling me about one of his guards being told off for not answering his radio whilst on 'sentry duty' at the top of the building. Upon checking his radio for serviceability, there was the giveaway clue as to why he had not answered it – a bullet was lodged in its side – he'd been saved by his equipment!

A few weeks later, 'Sid' left for home earlier than anticipated, with one in the throat. I never found out exactly how this affected him, but paralysis was mentioned in the same breath as his name.

My thoughts were starting to turn towards home and my family. Adam, my eldest, would be turning eight at Easter (about four weeks away) and I was due to fly home for some well-earned rest and recuperation (R&R).

Sunday mornings were my only downtime and it was on one such morning that I felt the world of Spirit directly touch mine for the first time since I had visited a spiritualist church some six months previously. There hadn't been much time for meditation, or anything spiritual, since my arrival in Basra, mainly due to the nightly rocket attacks and the weariness that sets in after a while.

I tried to have a long lie in that day but it was too hot. Feeling restless, I took a chair outside and sat down with a book. It wasn't long before the flies started to buzz around. They were a constant menace and I lost count of the times I slapped myself in the face trying to stave them off – it was useless. I gave up trying to read and moved. Not too far, though, as I didn't have my helmet or body armour with me. I moved just far enough, though, maybe 20 or 30 metres from my accommodation.

But even in my new position it was pointless trying to read. The flies and the heat were relentless. I stopped to take a drink of water from the plastic bottle that, since the weather had become hotter, had become a constant companion. My mind wandered and thoughts turned, once again, to home. What were the boys doing? Had my mum opened the doors yet at her second home, *The Pineapple Pub*, in Liverpool?

No was the answer. I checked my watch. In Basra time it was midday, but it was only 9am at home. It doesn't do to have too much spare time when you are away. I was starting to miss everybody.

Little did I know that Spirit was 'watching and listening'.

It was time to move back inside to the comfort of air con, but something right under my boot had caught my eye. Yes, I had stood on it.

Was that a ring pull from a can of Coke glinting in the sun? Whatever it was, I was drawn to it. If I'm one thing, that's nosey. Anybody else might have chosen to ignore the object but I just had to pick it up.

At first, I gave it a nudge with my boot, but that only served to shift more sand over the top of it. There was nothing else for it. I bent down and gave it a tug. It was a key ring, but not any old key ring. It took a while for the little trinket to register in my mind. What the hell was it? Finally, the penny dropped. It was a small, painted, typically Dutch clog. To anybody else, it would have been fairly unremarkable, I'm sure, but to me it was most definitely a message. At that moment, everything in my mind began to swirl and I suddenly felt a rush, almost like I was not in control of my own thoughts, or, more accurately, like somebody had taken control of them. I shuddered, as if somebody had walked right through me. It also felt like I was looking at the clog through somebody else's eyes. I knew whose eyes they were. For a split second, my maternal grandfather was with me and had completely enveloped me with his presence and love.

As mentioned, the key ring would have been totally insignificant to anyone else. Call it coincidence if you like, but I do not believe in happenstance – things always happen for a reason!

I had flown 3000 miles from home and had been given a room on a British military base in the desert. I chose that moment on that Sunday (something I had not done previously nor ever did again) to stop reading my book, move my chair and stand on a half buried, painted clog key ring 30-metres away from where I had originally been seated. Still think it's a coincidence?

What I haven't told you is that my maternal grandfather was Dutch. In fact, my paternal one was, too. They settled in Liverpool after WWII and raised families there. Not only that, clogs hold great significance for my family – we literally have them everywhere.

My father owned a restaurant called *Cloggs* that was adorned with trinkets related to its namesake. Even today, as I write this, there is a wall in my parents most recent establishment, *The Pineapple Pub* in Liverpool, that has pairs of clogs hanging from it, many of which are souvenirs brought over from Holland by visiting family or our frequent visits there.

Talking of Holland, my paternal Great, Great Grandmother, Maaike Neeltje Lagerwerf was a medium in Holland. Her daughter, Pietje Kaatje Luijten held seances at her own home and on to top of all of this, my paternal Great Aunt Neel, read tarot cards too!

Still think it's all a coincidence?

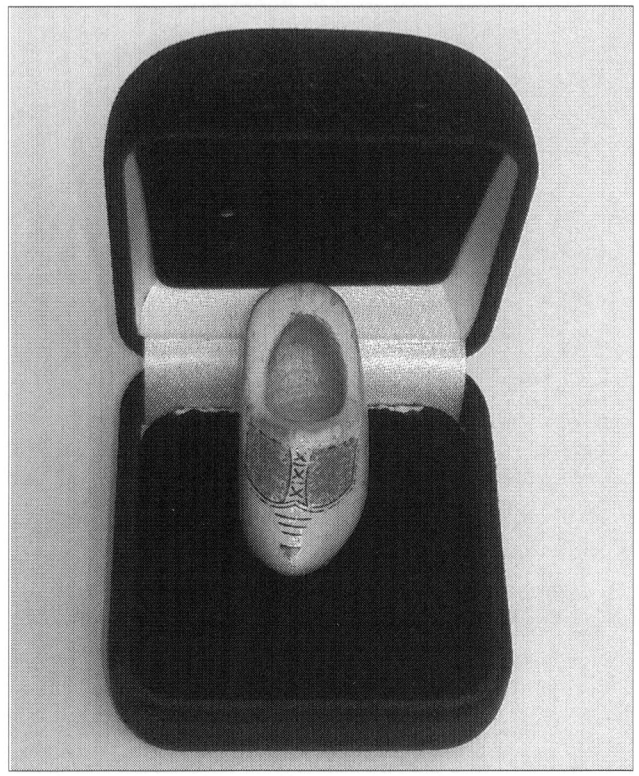

The Dutch clog I found in Iraq.

2. SPIRIT INSPIRATION

The spirit world inspires us in many different ways, but we don't always understand why or how. It's important for you to appreciate this if you are reading this guide and at the beginning of a spiritual journey but wish to communicate with Spirit more readily. Spirit communication should be a natural process. The only reason it may not feel this way is because we – or more accurately, our brains – get in the way.

We think far too much. Shoulda, Woulda, Coulda. We try to reason, plan, decipher and recall instead of just trying to 'be' – be in the moment. Rather than constantly going over old ground and living in the past, it's important to live in the now. We can plan to a certain degree, but what is the point?

"No battle plan ever survives first contact with the enemy," observed Helmuth von Moltke, a 19th century Prussian army leader. Live in the now and deal with what is happening in the now. Why? Because in the spirit world there is no time or distance.

I know there are times when you feel as though the spirit world has deserted you and left you feeling alone, but this is never really the case. Spirits are always around and will often let you feel their presence, but equally they will guide you gently through your days without necessarily making themselves known.

I am not always conscious of Spirit because I am busy concentrating on my earthly life, but I do remember one occasion when it let me know just how close it was.

My grandmother hated cooking but was very much a 'baker'. Her specialties were scones, jam tarts and apple pies, as well as Christmas and birthday cakes. At her house, Sundays were an absolute feast.

Long after she had passed, I decided to dedicate an afternoon to making pastry for an apple pie. As you will discover later, such tasks can be quite therapeutic and distracting, allowing us to enter an altered state of consciousness. I find that this is when Spirit steps in. On this particular day, I was working the pastry in the bowl and using a knife to scrape the excess off my fingers when I noticed a ring.

Now, I always take my rings off when making pastry, so spotting this was highly unusual, as was the style. It was an elongated oval shape made from silver. The stone in its centre was similar to a highly polished shell and was a kaleidoscope of colours. It wasn't my ring, but the ring my grandmother wore. I also saw her hands overshadowing mine. She was most definitely kneading the pastry with me.

That view of my grandmother's hands showed how natural the relationship with Spirit should be and how it can inspire us in a variety of ways outside mediumship.

Art, poetry, speaking, singing, writing music and producing lyrics for songs (poetry again) can all be greatly enhanced when we allow Spirit into our lives. Such inspiration is not always possible, though, due to our need to move to an altered state, but it's something we should strive towards.

3. UNDERSTANDING ENERGY

As Albert Einstein once said, *"Energy cannot be created or destroyed, it can only be changed from one form to another."*

Meanwhile, Nikola Tesla, the Serbian-American inventor, engineer and physicist, was quoted as saying, *"If you want to find the secrets of the universe, think in terms of energy, frequency and vibration."*

Everything, including our own body, is made up of energy, which is vibrating at different frequencies. That said, it seems logical to wonder whether sound frequencies affect us or not. Frequencies do affect frequencies, much like mixing ingredients together impacts the overall flavour of a meal.

From a spiritual perspective, I prefer to describe us as energy enjoying a human experience. I also believe that our experiences are not limited to the human form or this planet.

If you feel brave enough, have a look at the 'Many-Worlds Theory' or the 'Double-Slit Experiment'. It may change your understanding of what you think you know. Have you forgotten that 500 years ago we thought the world was flat? Imagine what you might know tomorrow.

You may decide that this all sounds a bit too complicated, but in reality you are already a master of understanding the energy and frequencies around you.

Understanding changes in energy is intrinsic to your development as a medium. How many times have you been aware of an atmosphere in a room when you have walked into it? How many times have you felt as though you were being watched in an empty room, or sensed the presence of somebody immediately as they walked in silently behind you?

You can see already that you are sensitive to changes around you – making you aware of such energy is all part of my teachings!

Have you heard of the frequency 432 Hz? Known as Verdi's 'A' (after the classical composer), it's an alternative tuning that is mathematically consistent with the universe.

So, what has music and its vibrational frequency got to do with your mediumship? Music doesn't necessarily come in here, but when you're working as a medium you constantly change the vibration at which you work. The closer you get to working at the same frequency as the universe, the clearer your communication becomes with it. Remember, we are all part of the universe.

How many times have you heard yourself say, "We are not on the same wavelength" when referring to another individual?

Have you ever listened to music when you are cheerful and zooming along in your car? You resonate with its beat. However, upon reaching a jam or traffic lights, which seem to take forever to move or change, your mood takes a nosedive and the music now seems at odds with how you feel. You may feel frustrated or anxious about being restricted and look for music that reflects this. You may even opt for silence.

When working with Spirit, this will happen quite often. You may resonate with one person and their loved ones in Spirit, but then find the next person you encounter is on a totally different frequency. This is perfectly normal, but to understand this energy work further, you first need to comprehend what is happening inside your head.

4. ALTERED STATES OF CONSCIOUSNESS

Understanding brain waves allows us to alter our state of consciousness and tap into our abilities.

Four brain wave frequencies will be discussed here: Beta, Alpha, Theta and Delta.

Normal adult brain waves

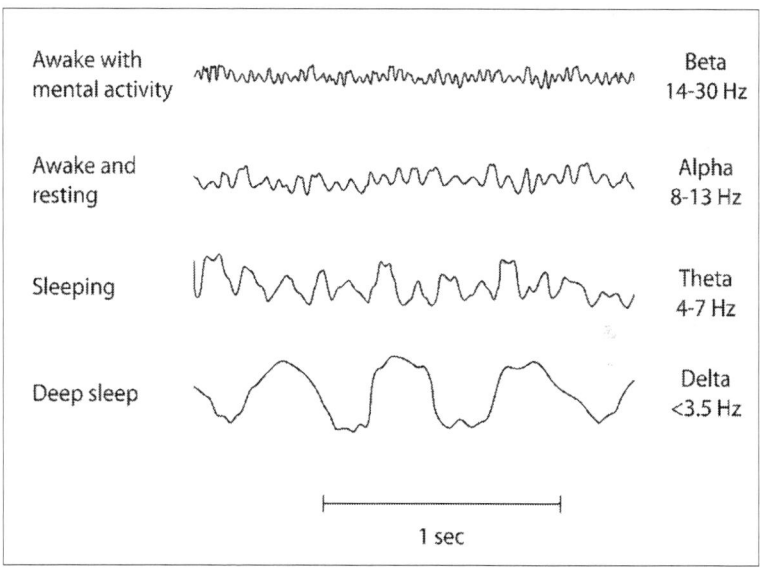

Figure 1 - Normal adult brain waves

By consciously altering these brain waves we can tap into new means of exploring different modes of awareness.

Beta waves

The Beta wave is the most closely related to our conscious mind. Here, the brain waves are cycling between 14 to 30 Hz. Beta brain waves utilise our physical senses and, as a result, our mediumistic faculties become muted. This is because exterior stimuli dominate our thoughts and actions and suppress any inspiration from Spirit.

Many people live their entire lives in the Beta mode. In fact, the moment they find themselves slipping into an Alpha state of awareness they grow uncomfortable and do something to stop their momentary transition into inner reflection. They turn on the television, call their friends, read mindless material, partake in drugs or alcohol – or simply go to bed and drift into a dreamless sleep.

Such people tend to be unhappy with themselves or the direction their life is taking, or they may be fearful about confronting something within that may require painful changes. These are also the people who do not listen to their inner voice.

Alpha waves

Brain waves in the Alpha state of awareness oscillate between 8 and 13 Hz. This is where we tend to 'drift off'. Daydreaming or meditating takes us very much into the Alpha state. This state of mind is often linked to the three creative 'Bs' - bed, bath and bus – for we feel relaxed in places like these and can reflect a bit on issues at hand and allow Spirit to inspire us with information, ideas or solutions. Your eyes do not need to be closed, but the mind does need to be liberated. This isn't hard to do. Just let the inner chatter quieten down for a bit, and you'll be amazed at the things that start coming to you.

As individuals, we do not want to be in a perpetual Alpha state. Daydreamers spend a lot of time in this mode. Some can even get caught up in it and suffer from ADHD (Attention Deficit Hyperactivity Disorder), since they can't focus for long on their physical reality before returning to their wispy state of reflection and dreaming. However, an easy and perpetual access to this state is great for writers, poets and artists.

The point here, of course, is to consciously direct your awareness to each state until you can reach deep Theta. This, as most people will discover, is done through meditation or via learning how to bounce in and out of the sleep state upon waking (the hypnogogic state).

5. DISCOVERING THE SELF THROUGH ALTERED STATES OF CONSCIOUSNESS

Just as musicians need to constantly practice their musical scales, we mediums need to meditate – and not very many do this regularly enough.

Meditating often, as well as working as a medium – whether that's for demonstrations of clairvoyance or private one-to-one readings – will help you receive from Spirit or simply calm the mind. During a meditation, we evolve and grow and Spirit teaches us.

Meditation is *not* thinking about nothing because this is impossible. We are consciousness and whether we are still physically alive or not, that consciousness lives on. Meditation is about controlling our mind, rather than allowing the so-called 'monkey mind' to run riot.

Buddhists believe that the spirit and the mind should move as one – not unlike the way a horse and its rider move together. If you have ever seen an inexperienced rider out of sync with their horse, you'll know it looks pretty painful. Your mind is the rider and your spirit is the horse. Learn to move as one and life will suddenly become an easier journey.

Meditation isn't easy, but another method of finding that inner peace and tranquillity is through yoga. Everybody I have ever spoken to (and I agree with them) say they feel 'at one' or peaceful after a workout. Have a go, as it will help you understand the notion of oneness, which will definitely improve your mediumistic development.

Try this as an experiment. Attempt to clear your mind, and if things do pop in acknowledge them and allow them to move on. You could even try and put those thoughts and ideas into a virtual balloon and send it skywards. When you know you won't be disturbed, simply try and clear your mind for 10-15 minutes.

Now pick up your phone and scroll through a few social media posts or emails. Put your device down and attempt to clear your mind again, as you did before. Do you notice a slight change in the focus of your attention? Did you detect a change in your consciousness or awareness?

"Of course," you might argue, "what else would I expect?" That is your brain switching between Alpha and Beta waves and back to Alpha again. You do not have to understand it to know that you have to 'get back into the zone' before working for Spirit.

Top Tip #1: Clear your mind totally prior to working for Spirit.

You have to start as you mean to go on. Mediumship is an extension of your own spirituality and should be part of your way of life – not something you do on a Friday night for two hours.

As my boys were growing up and starting to stay up later, I would wait for things to settle down in their bedroom and then sit in the dark and clear my head. This is the first stage. You don't necessarily have to follow this with a meditation, simply get used to sitting in your own company, without external stimuli, and feeling comfortable.

We are so used to beeps, pings and buzzes that it has become almost second nature to grab a device simply to check that somebody 'likes' what we said earlier. Half the time, we do not even realise we're doing it.

Think back to a decade or so ago, before the advent of the smartphone and social media, and to when texts and emails weren't an everyday occurrence in our busy lives.

Imagine that I am holding a conversation with you when a letter drops onto my doormat. How would you feel if I then proceeded to open and read it before composing a handwritten reply and popping out to buy a stamp so I could immediately post it?

The number of times I have been in somebody's company when they have done all of the above, but just with an email or text. Admittedly, it can all be done in the blink of an eye and if a letter did drop through the front door it would probably be ignored, but is it any less rude to answer emails or texts while holding a conversation? We are constantly being distracted.

When did you last give somebody your undivided attention? We have become so overloaded with information and most of it is useless, but we still absorb it to the point where we are in touch with our inner self less and less.

Learn to get into the habit of going somewhere quiet and clearing your mind. This is a discipline and one you will need in order to develop your mediumship, which is a life-long learning process. There isn't an app in the world that will do this for you. There is no quick fix.

Also, try getting into the routine of putting your devices on silent and maybe checking them periodically during your working day, rather than every 30 seconds when another piece of junk mail flies into your inbox.

Personally, only my ringtone sounds on my phone. This helps me achieve so much more in my day and also improves my concentration levels. Secondly, I really do not feel like I am missing out on much by using this approach. In fact, I am gaining because I notice my inner voice much more - try it.

Moving on from sitting in the quiet, you need to learn how to concentrate the mind and get it to do what you want. Your mind and spirit should be as one.

If you already meditate regularly and are happy with your own routine, that's fine, or, if you wish to listen to a guided meditation then please go to www.theroomnextdoor.com.

Trusting the World of Spirit

Did you fall asleep during that exercise or fail to keep your concentration?

It isn't as easy as you think, is it? You may well eventually develop your own meditation techniques or follow other ones, but the thrust of what I am trying to help you achieve here is for you to simply make time for yourself and to 'go within'.

You can employ this process during your day-to-day routine when seeking answers – it's not just for mediumship. It can help with all manner of things, and if you can't dedicate 30 minutes to yourself a few times each week then what is the world coming to? You should be strengthening your connection to your inner self (your spirit) in order to gain strength in real times of need. We never know when we might need to call upon our inner self to guide us in our daily lives.

When my youngest son was 14, apart from the normal teenage growing pains, he seemed quite unsettled in himself, particularly at school. He eventually told us that he wanted to leave that school and go to another one, which many of his friends attended. Charlie and I were in a real quandary about what to do. Our son was in a good school, was performing well and the staff and his peers held him in high regard. Despite this, he kept pushing to leave. This went on and on for around six months and Charlie felt that moving schools was the wrong thing to do. She is very intuitive, too, but we all still need to trust our inner compass sometimes. If you have no idea how to get in touch with yourself, how can you trust yourself?

I decided to wait until I knew I would not be disturbed and rather than let my head get in the way and confuse everything, I chose to go 'within'. That evening, I found a quiet space, cleared my head and let go of any thoughts. I didn't try anything miraculous but simply attempted to be 'in the moment'. I have no idea how long I'd been sat in my chair when I noticed something on the floor. I went to pick it up and as I reached down, I heard, "do nothing" accompanied by a vision of my son. That was my 'burning bush' moment. It chimes with the time I bent down to retrieve the painted Dutch clog key ring from the desert sand in Iraq. So, what is it about picking things up, I hear you ask?

Well, absolutely nothing.

It is the fact that I was distracted and my brain wasn't actually thinking about the issue at hand (despite me trying to clear my mind), which, in turn, allowed me to receive the intention of Spirit. Whilst I was sidetracked, Spirit stepped in. That is how difficult it is to get your brain out of the way sometimes, no matter how hard you try.

We try and evaluate too much. We try and think things through and make logical assumptions about illogical feelings. We are so used to being in control.

Regarding my son, he is fine now. The way he was feeling actually had nothing to do with the school he was at but something personal to him and things soon passed. Being 14 did not help either, but he is much happier in his own skin now. Doing nothing went against the grain, but it proved to be the right course to take.

Top Tip #2 : Trust Spirit

---

6. HEALTH KICKS AND EARTHLY RESPONSIBILITIES

Now that you have a better understanding about what is happening with you regarding your mediumship, we need to look inwards once again.

Many mediums do suffer with health issues, but Spirit 'lifts' them to allow them to work. If you happen to be blessed with good health, this will stand you in good stead for your spiritual work. However, you do still need to look after yourself.

Getting the best out of your mediumship

Diet

Prior to working with Spirit, ensure you eat something to keep you going. Do not dine on something that is too heavy and allow plenty of time to allow your digestive system to 'go to work' too.

We all know what happens if we eat a heavy lunch and then try and go back to work or concentrate – siesta time.

Working for Spirit requires discipline. If junk food is your God, think again. As my gift has developed, I have started to crave food that is not too heavy and doesn't make me feel sluggish, but this does not mean that you cannot treat yourself every now and again.

After working for Spirit for prolonged periods, your appetite will skyrocket and you will burn up calories at an amazing rate, but only for a few hours. Feeding your appetite is one thing but eating the wrong foods and then going to bed (as much of your work could be in the evenings) is a dietary nightmare and your body (including your waistline) will not thank you for it.

Energy

Your work will naturally involve an exchange of energy and this will affect you. Care must be taken to safeguard and maintain the energy you use, as some events will draw an awful lot from you.

It's difficult if you have other considerations, such as a full-time job or family to take care of. Don't become engulfed in spiritual work to the detriment of your private life. A balance is required.

Don't be surprised if your spiritual work suffers. You can be physically drained for mediumship, but if you are mentally tired your work will falter.

I cannot stress enough the importance of safeguarding your energy, but just as when you were a child and were told not to do something but did it anyway, you'll be just as tempted to do the opposite of what's good for you when it comes to your energy. You will find out where your own limits lie by learning the hard way.

Fitness and grounding

To help with your new dietary regimen, taking in some air or regular exercise needs to be part of your daily routine. Although I do not thank him for it on cold, rainy days, my dog needs a daily walk and I also feel better for it.

I am not saying buy a dog, especially if you do not have time to care for one, but if you do have one it won't complain if you start taking it for a stroll more than usual.

Look at some fitness websites for information about getting in shape. If exercise is not part of your life already, check in with your doctor for professional guidance. Your general wellbeing and your mediumship will definitely improve as a result.

Spiritual work takes its toll and will leave you feeling elated, tired and giddy, as well as a little spaced-out sometimes. Get yourself out into the open and into nature. When was the last time you listened to the birds singing? They sing all the time and I am sure you do hear them, but you are probably so wrapped up in your own mind that you don't hear what they are saying. What about the rustle of the leaves in the trees? Even the babbling brook has something to say. Getting out into nature will help you to relate to the physical world around you, which in turn will centre you.

On warm summer days, I often walk around the local fields with bare feet, in order to help ground myself. Recently I felt inspired to grab hold of an oak tree. I imagined everything that was bothering me draining out of my arms, trickling down the tree's trunk and going into the roots and way, way down into the earth.

You can try any method you like for grounding yourself, but it is something you need to do every now and again.

Sleep

A lot of the information surrounding your health and wellbeing will help you live a more spiritual existence, but a good night's sleep is essential. I did mention that you can be physically but not mentally tired when performing mediumship. Quietening the mind before bed will aid a restful sleep and put you on top form for doing your mediumistic work. Please try and make this part of your lifestyle, too. You will thank yourself for it.

Alcohol

Everything in moderation. There is certainly enough medical evidence around to keep us well informed about the effects of alcohol on the body. Alcohol and mediumship are not compatible. Do not mix your spirits!

Your earthly responsibilities

I mentioned earlier about balancing your personal life with your spiritual work. People want to see us when they are not in work, i.e. in the evenings or at weekends. This makes our working lives slightly antisocial. Added to this, you might work full-time and have a family to raise. Your spouse may work long hours, too. Are you seeing the picture I am painting?

Development circles and workshops will often be held at weekends or in the evenings, and you may be just too tired to attend them.

Sometimes, the hardest part about this work is a potential lack of empathy from your partner. I remember one lady paying a deposit to attend one of my workshops only to pull out at the last minute. She told me her husband had decided to go fishing, which meant she couldn't attend. She dropped the course to save any marital strife.

Expect to be given a hard time in some aspects of your life because this work will grip you – there is no other feeling like it. Be prepared to stand your ground but remember there has to be some give and take in any situation.

Top Tip #3: COMMITMENT, COMMITMENT, COMMITMENT

---

7. CREATING YOUR SACRED SPACE AND GROUND RULES

During controlled experiments, scientists found they achieved their best results while testing subjects for ESP abilities while there were few or no distractions. Lights were dimmed, the rooms were windowless and auditory and visual stimuli were removed where possible.

As mentioned, yoga helps us feel at one. Although it can be performed at home, it's best to do a class elsewhere because this will help you escape the distractions that take up valuable 'space' in your head.

I have lost count of the amount of times I have been disturbed by mail dropping through the front door and the dog barking. There are only so many precautions you can take to ensure you have some peace and quiet.

Top Tip #4: Create a dedicated space for yourself.

This isn't just the space around you; it is also the space in your head. We need to achieve those Alpha waves I spoke about earlier.

Many years ago, I would drive in the rush hour straight from work to the Open Circle at my local church. I never understood why it took me about an hour before I could truly feel the presence of Spirit. Only after finishing work early one week and relaxing prior to Circle did it suddenly dawn on me what was happening. Most of the time when I arrived at church I was still thoroughly planted in this world and had not changed my own vibration in order to be ready to work with Spirit. In essence, until I settled down, my brain was still going crazy with Beta waves. When I finally felt calm I was able to move to an altered state, such as Alpha or Theta waves.

These days, prior to doing any work for Spirit, I conduct the meditation I've provided a link to in this book and allow myself to open up. I also gather my team of spirit guides and inspirers and thank God for letting me work with the highest and the best, as well as showing gratitude for the messages I'll receive on behalf of the people I'm about to work for.

Churches or places where people go to receive messages of love and inspiration from Spirit should have a Medium's Room, where you can prepare yourself. If the one you attend doesn't have this facility, ask for it!

You need to control the space you are about to work in, as unfortunately it is not all love and light out there.

You have to live in the physical world but you also need to set boundaries. Even when you're working in somebody else's home, you can ask for your protectors to bless the space and create your own little bit of heaven to work in.

Going to somebody else's house to perform private readings is another matter. In my early years, I would travel far and wide to my clients. There were many occasions when I wish I hadn't.

Example #1

Back in 2009, I was invited to do some readings at someone's home. It was a bonus that I had a day off and it was during the day, which saved me waiting until the evening, when most people want their readings.

The other bonus was that the client's house wasn't very far away from where I lived. When I arrived at the small terrace, I noted nothing unusual about the property or the street.

Having knocked on the door, I had to wait longer than usual for someone to answer. As a rule, people who are waiting for a visitor hover close by. But eventually the door creaked open and a young woman in her early twenties beckoned me in. Enquiring whether she was Joan, the lady I had called to see, the woman simply said, "No." I

Creating Your Sacred Space and Ground Rules

have encountered clients being deliberately scant with information in the past, so her evasiveness was not totally out of place.

As I was ushered towards the back of the house, it dawned on me that the place was eerily quiet and bordering on musty, as if there had been a lack of airflow for some time.

Most clients offer me a drink or ask whether I have any particular preferences for where I work. I have found myself in bedrooms, spaces under stairs, kitchens, living rooms and even conservatories or garden sheds. On this occasion, I was seated in the back room. Having arrived in bright sunshine, it took a while for my eyes to adjust, as the room was in total darkness.

It is no lie when people talk about using 'the element of surprise', because if anybody had wanted to cause me harm that day they would have definitely had the upper hand.

A tealight candle burned on a low table and beyond that I couldn't really see much else except the outline of a body seated on a chair in the shadows created by the candle's flickering flame. I was really starting to wonder what I had let myself in for.

If you refer back to the first paragraph of this chapter, you will see where my client was perhaps coming from. I knew this was a test, as I have seen people take pictures off walls and hide items, removing any clues that fraudulent mediums might use to gain insights into the lives of their clients, but this was beyond anything I had experienced previously.

What my client had failed to realise is that as part of my training I have performed readings wearing a blindfold, in order to ensure the efficacy of my work. Proving myself was never going to be a problem, but – ego aside – I could have really put myself in danger.

Amongst many other things I picked up about my client was that she was expecting a baby. The whole dark room thing was starting to make even more sense – she was obviously trying to hide her pregnancy, thus testing my abilities. Take it from me, don't ever allow yourself to get stuck in such a situation.

On this occasion, things turned out fine. As it happened, the pregnant lady had an antenatal appointment later that day and I even offered her a lift as it was on my way home.

My message? Keep yourself safe!

If you can afford it, having a space of your own, such as an office, is ideal.

A lot of people work from home but this does carry its own issues, especially concerning work-life balance. Having an office or shop carries overheads but it will provide you with a dedicated space to build up your energies within.

The idea of having a sacred space relates to others, too. You will have heard about people who give 'messages' in supermarkets, bars or in the street. They may well have been working with Spirit for many years and might not need to prepare as much as you, but it is not just about being in the right space yourself, it is all about your recipient.

> Top Tip #5: Do not give people messages in public places without their permission.

Not only is it an invasion of their privacy, the recipient might not be in the right space to hear it. They may have been thinking about seeing a medium, but it's important to let them do this on their own terms.

8. FIRST STAGES

Sensitivity

Sensitivity is something that we all rely on as mediums and it determines how easy we find it to communicate with Spirit.

Some of us are born naturally sensitive to the physical world and are, therefore, aware of subtle changes in energy and vibration. You may pick up on the feelings of others more readily or a certain location or a building might 'say' things to you. It's possible you don't understand what those things are or what they mean, but you are still aware of them.

Please don't assume that because you are sensitive to the physical world you will automatically be an amazing medium. Your sensitivity simply means that you have a bit of a head start. You will still need to work just as hard as everybody else, because Spirit WILL challenge you in different ways to help you grow.

On the other hand, you may feel that you are not very sensitive at all. This won't be the case. We all have various vibrational sensitivities and when we feel we have nothing to offer it may be that our particular skillset is different. You may excel in areas where others fear to tread.

Champion sprinters cannot be champion marathon runners, and you will eventually find your own true vocation.

Before you begin

Prior to any work with Spirit, you will need to protect yourself. This can be as simple as saying a prayer, asking for protection and surrounding yourself in white light. You might even ask for specific angels to watch over you, but whatever you choose, please ensure you do protect yourself.

There are many ways you might connect to Spirit without actually realising how you have achieved this. For any beginner, there needs to be a somewhat mechanical process, which I will talk you through. Even if you feel accomplished in your ability, read on.

Attunement

This is about changing your vibration. Yes, the same vibration we were talking about earlier. This connects you with the spirit world and from your perspective gives Spirit permission to come forward. Some of you may experience having Spirit around you all day, but maintaining a strict work schedule will work wonders and keep you on top form.

Blend

A very important part of working with Spirit is blending your energy with that of your communicator. You should feel as one. Remember how I spoke earlier about my grandmother working with me whilst I made an apple pie? Your mediumship should not feel as though Spirit is shouting to you from the other side of the room, almost detached, but there are reasons why it may feel this way.

Communication

Once blended, you will be ready to communicate with the spirit world, which should inspire you. Many clients will want answers to specific questions, but do not force anything. If somebody does have a question, let them voice it but then let the issue go. The more you 'think', the more you will tie yourself up in knots. Working for Spirit is about feeling.

As you know, for a connection to be made, a medium needs to raise his/her vibration to match that of the spirit world. Prior to doing any work, as already stated, you should be in the right space.

The meditation you performed earlier at www.theroomnextdoor.co.uk can be repeated before embarking on any spiritual work.

First Stages

Basic mediation exercise

Here is that same exercise in a basic format. It is designed to allow you to go through each stage. Read through the whole exercise then try and work through it practically.

Ensure that you are sitting comfortably and in an upright position with your eyes closed.

a. Imagine a white light shining brightly in the area of your third eye (located in the centre of your forehead).

b. Imagine that light moving downwards towards the centre of your being and resting in the area associated with your solar plexus.

c. Allow the light to emanate from the centre of your being upwards through your torso towards your head, along your arms and also downwards through your legs and feet into the earth.

d. Allow the light to consume you.

e. Finally, allow the white light to rise upwards towards the heavens. Let it keep rising until it meets a similar white light spiralling down from the heavens towards you.

Stages (a)-(d) should take fifteen minutes at least. The idea is that by following the light you will rest your mind and bring it under your control, rather than letting it control you.

Stage (e) could take at least another five to 10 minutes.

This is one method of connecting with Spirit, and with time and practice it becomes less mechanical. It's something I always do prior to working.

Once you have achieved this state, imagine the spirit world around you and invite it into your 'bubble' – which is in fact your auric field.

You can also practice this exercise with a work partner. Make your auric field as large or as small as you wish by expanding it like a balloon and then ask your partner to walk into it. When they do this, you should be able to sense the change in energy. Keeping your eyes closed, your partner could walk towards your front, back or sides, with you indicating where they are at that time simply by using your senses.

You could try this with both male and female work partners, using your senses to establish who it is approaching you. Indicate with your left hand if they are female and with your right if they are male. The whole point of this exercise is for you to understand the different feelings that come with somebody entering your auric field. It also answers the question regarding how you know when Spirit is present and how you know the sex of a person without seeing them. Basically, you will just know!

N.B. All future meditations will be based upon stages (a)-(e) and will be a variation on a theme thereafter.

9. READY, STEADY

Now that you have mastered how to prepare yourself and the space you work in, you will have already opened your awareness to the world of Spirit. But what about the people you intend to work for – your clients? As a medium, communicating with Spirit may feel like second nature, but your client might not have spoken to a medium before and may even have heard scary stories from friends.

The work we do is primarily subjective. By this I mean that whatever you tell somebody during a reading, how they feel at that time will determine what they make of it. You are only ever as good as your last reading.

It's important to understand that we don't just grab messages from Spirit, dump them on people and then relax as proud as punch. That would be letting the ego play its part. There is a three-way relationship between you, your client and Spirit. The energy flows like AC electricity between the three of you, which aids the communication. And just like with electricity, the energy flow between you and your recipients will follow the path of least resistance.

One lady I tried to read for either would not or could not settle down. As a rule, if I am working with a client and they are saying no to me continually, it's not simply a matter of me being wrong or not connecting to them for some reason. There is often something larger at play. It could be anything.

As a medium, you have got to be alert at all times to the flow of the energy in the room. Is it moving? Is it staccato? Is it totally blocked?

Eventually, I stopped the reading and asked her if she was OK, as I was sensing the block. The lady was very reluctant to answer until I laid it on the line and said that after 15 minutes her reading should be in full swing, but she remained distracted. She then blurted out that she had not put enough money in the parking meter and was afraid she would get a ticket. This is absolutely true and proves how something as simple as worrying about a fine can affect a reading.

Being wise to such situations now, I keep my radar switched on at all times. Spirit had most definitely taught me a lesson because not long after that, a lady came into my shop and asked if I was available to do a reading. I was, but something made me ask her if she was free.

"What do you mean?" she asked.

"Do you have time to sit with me, relax and enjoy your reading?" I asked.

"Well, I've left my kids with my mother in a coffee shop and thought I would dive in for a quick reading with you."

Voila!

I asked the lady if she could possibly come back when she could afford to spend the time with me, as she wouldn't benefit from a reading right now, as the anxiety she felt about her children being with her mother would block anything I had for her.

I never saw her again.

Prior to starting your reading, you won't know what your client is bringing into the room.

It could be any of the following:

    a.   Anxiety derived from whether their loved one will come through for them or not. Similarly, they may not wish to encounter a certain person.

    b.   Some clients arrive with only one thing on their mind. If their loved one does not mention it, the reading is written off. That one thing could be the communicator's name, a special name they had for each other or even a code word that was agreed upon beforehand.

    c.   The client hasn't grieved.

d. The potential communicator's physical body hasn't been found and it has not been proven that they have actually passed over to Spirit.

e. There may have been suspicious circumstances surrounding the passing. Some clients look for such things to be proven/disproven because they are overcome with grief and need closure (see c).

...Go!

The following list of checks is not prescriptive, but, depending on your client's experience, you may pick 'n' mix what's on it to suit your own requirements.

Believe me when I tell you that people holding in emotion will be the biggest block to your mediumship. It may not be grief that is the block.

Your client may have had a long journey and need the bathroom or simply be frazzled from nerves. You never know. I often ask my clients to take a seat before kicking things off with a general chat. I always offer them something to drink, but why not try some of the following:

a. Ask if they have ever had a reading before. If the answer is yes, go to (c). If the answer is no, proceed to (b).

b. Reassure them that there is nothing to worry about. There is no bad news and spirits are not there to ruin their day, as they come through on a love vibration and love comes from the heart. For the best communication, we need their heart to be healed, but if it is still on the mend, we can still work with that.

I use the analogy that a broken heart is like a bottle of champagne that has been shaken while the cork is still secured and holding everything in. The last thing we want to happen is for that cork to be ejected, with the liquid (emotion) soaking us all.

c. Explain how you work and that you cannot force Spirit to come through, nor can you stop it. If your client has somebody in mind, ask them to send their thoughts out to Spirit, as communication is what you are all there for.

d. Tell your client what evidence you will receive from Spirit as proof of their survival (see the following chapter).

e. Ensure that if your client does not understand something you have said, they must tell you and allow you to clarify it.

10. MEET THE 'CLAIRS'

So many people within the world of mediumship throw around certain clichés or buzzwords, while everybody else seems to be playing catch-up with the latest thinking. However, not a lot has really changed since the advent of modern spiritualism on March 31st, 1848 with the Fox sisters. Through a series of raps and taps on the walls of their home in Hydesville, New York, they were able to establish for themselves that life does exist beyond the physical realm.

Sensing the world of Spirit falls into six main areas, which are commonly referred to as the 'Clairs'.

1. Clairvoyance (Clear Seeing)

Clairvoyance comes from the French words 'clair' (clear) and 'voir' (to see). Essentially, this is a person's ability to see things that aren't necessarily visible to the naked eye. Clairvoyants receive extrasensory impressions and symbols in the form of 'inner sight' or mental images, which are perceived without the aid of the physical eyes. I mentioned altered states of consciousness earlier and how some people might begin to receive information when in the Alpha state but then quickly revert to the Beta state because they are not at ease with receiving it in the form of clairvoyance. Being an accomplished medium takes a lot of practice, as it's not easy to enter such altered states 'on demand', hence the need to meditate as much as possible.

2. Clairaudience (Clear Hearing)

Perceiving sounds and/or words and extrasensory noise broadcast from a spiritual or ethereal realm, in the form of an 'inner ear' or mental tone, which are perceived without the aid of the physical ears and are beyond the limitations of ordinary time and space. Again, these tones and vibrations are easier to perceive in an Alpha state. Most mediums work with both clairvoyance and clairaudience.

3. Clairsentience (Clear Sensing)

Perceiving information by a 'feeling' within the whole body, without the input of any outer stimuli.

Spirit will build for you an encyclopedia of knowledge and symbols, depending on how they wish to work with you. My messages sometimes come in the form of feeling ill. For example, more often than not, if my mouth feels dry, in a certain way, I know that somebody had passed with cancer and what I'm experiencing is indicative of the dryness caused by the administering of morphine. However, this sensation is not to be confused with Clairgustance, which I'll discuss further on.

I have also felt pressure in my head from a spirit person who passed to Spirit with a brain tumour.

4. Claircognizance (Clear Knowing)

Put simply, this is when you become aware of something about somebody that you couldn't possibly have known beforehand.

My most marked example of this took place when I was invited to a house to perform what I believed were going to be a series of private readings. Upon my arrival, I was greeted and shown to the front room of the house. I was then asked if I could read for all three people at the same time. It transpired that they were siblings – one brother and two sisters.

As I entered the room, I knew instantly that the house had belonged to their mother and had been bequeathed to one of the daughters. We could argue all day about how exactly I came by this information, but I had no prior knowledge of it before entering the house.

5. Clairalience (Clear Smelling)

This is a wonderful way of sensing something, especially if it carries further significance. People who don't consider themselves to be mediums often report smelling lavender, roses or even bread being baked. Where does your own mind take you when I tell you to think about tar, fresh paint or the smell of freshly cut grass? Even without a spirit communicator, you could well be transported back to your own childhood or a special place of significance. Imagine what a spirit communicator could tell you from just one smell.

6. Clairgustance (Clear Tasting)

Many mediums might taste alcohol, tobacco or some other strong taste. Certain mediums might have very good Clairgustance and may detect more subtle flavours. As with Clairalience, think about some of your own favourite tastes and what they mean to you. Are they connected to a job or a memorable event?

All of the 'Clairs' tell a story to you and you just need to be tuned into it. Read on to see how you can take your natural senses to the next level.

11. COLLECTING EVIDENCE

Memories	Places	Jewellery	REASON
Vacations	Food	Occupation	Habits
Relationship	Personality	Ailments	Mannerisms

Figure 2. Table of evidence

The table above (which you can copy and use in your own work) contains 'points of evidence' and can be used as a guide whenever you are working with Spirit.

Whilst I cannot take such a table with me during a stage show, Spirit will use different references or 'cues' to gain attention. The table is simply one method I teach to help my students gain an understanding of the workings of Spirit. It's by no means prescriptive and it's also not a checklist. Anybody can run through a list and count it as evidence, but we want to bring your client's loved ones to life in the room and let them feel the love of Spirit. There is no better feeling than when somebody leaves a reading saying, "I felt my dad/brother/mother in the room with me."

Your client should feel part of the communication and feel the love that is intended for them.

Working through the evidence

Use this flow diagram in conjunction with the previous table to aid your Spirit communication.

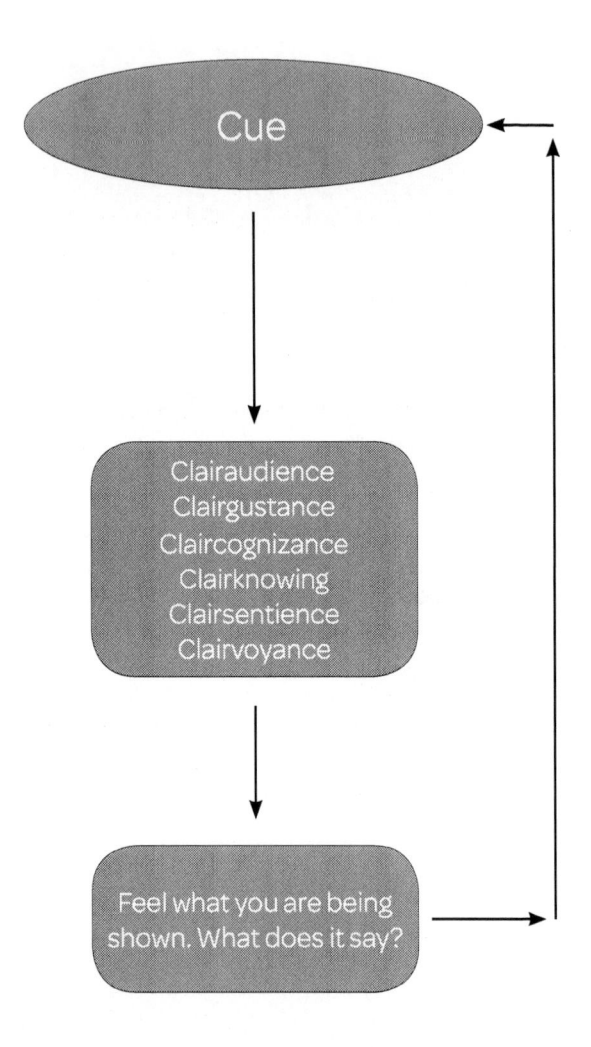

```
        ┌─────────┐
        │   Cue   │ ◄──┐
        └────┬────┘    │
             ▼         │
    ┌──────────────┐   │
    │ Clairaudience│   │
    │ Clairgustance│   │
    │Claircognizance│  │
    │ Clairknowing │   │
    │ Clairsentience│  │
    │ Clairvoyance │   │
    └──────┬───────┘   │
           ▼           │
    ┌──────────────┐   │
    │Feel what you │   │
    │are being     │───┘
    │shown. What   │
    │does it say?  │
    └──────────────┘
```

Figure 3 - Flow diagram of evidence

The 'cue' is what Spirit makes you aware of through your senses, and there will always be a feeling that comes with it. You might be shown an item, as you will see later in the worked example. What does the feeling that accompanies the item say to you? Is it sadness, happiness, joy, love, anxiety, concern, or something else?

There might not be an item, just a feeling. Every time you are given an item and/or a feeling, 'feel into it' around the area of your solar plexus and see what it says. Feed that feeling back into the flow chart and be aware of what comes next. This is known as an iterative process. From one item or feeling, a whole message will evolve.

When it comes to putting the theory into practice, one human organ can and often does scupper a whole message and send you into a spin. That organ is your brain. While it's a wonderful organ, it will try to get in the way and make logical thoughts out of illogical feelings. Remember, the message is for your recipient, not you, and what might make perfect sense to your client might leave you feeling totally confused. It's best to leave your brain at home for any work with Spirit.

Working example

Reading through the scenario below will help you gain a clearer understanding of how to deal with situations that may arise in your own work.

As you settle down with your recipient and ask Spirit to step forward using the previous exercises, you become aware of a man in your auric field.

There is a distinct feeling of 'Dad' with him. Looking at your table, your eyes rest upon the word 'occupation'. Always go for the very first word you are drawn to, as this is inspiration from Spirit. Now feel that word.

'Dad' has drawn very close to you and you become aware of something in your hand – a screwdriver. This is known as *Subjective Viewing*. Alternatively, you might see 'Dad' standing with your recipient while holding the tool in his hand. This is known as *'Objective Viewing'*. However you are seeing 'Dad', now use the flow diagram. The screwdriver is your visual 'cue'.

You will find the next few stages very mechanical and formal, but they do work. As you develop, you won't even notice the seamless transition between the steps, and you will develop your own style of delivery, too.

The conversation goes like this:

You: "I sense a man here from Spirit and he feels like your dad to me. Can I confirm that your dad is in Spirit?"

Client: "Yes, he is."

You: "I see him holding a screwdriver in his hand. Why would he be holding this?"

Some clients will deny the screwdriver and let you do the work, but the majority will try and work something out for you. The screwdriver might not make any sense at all to them. It is your role to sort out the evidence.

Now take the screwdriver, place it in the area of your solar plexus and FEEL it. What is it saying to you? Do not think about it at all. Concentrate all your activity around your solar plexus.

Feeling into the screwdriver could produce another visual 'cue' for you.

Dad is standing in a doorway and you see him tightening up screws on a door hinge.

Your brain might say: "Dad was a handyman and was always fixing things around the home." OR: "Dad was a carpenter and 'hanging' doors was part of his job."

WRONG!

You are now allowing your brain to guess what the cues mean.

In your mind's eye, take a step back and look at the bigger picture.

Alternatively, say to 'Dad', "Show me more."

As you step back, you notice you are in a living room surrounded by people.

Taking a further step back, you notice what appears to be TV cameras.

There is nothing wrong with now saying:

"I see your dad holding a screwdriver, but I also see a room full of people and what looks like TV cameras. Does this make sense to you?"

Client: "Yes."

Carry on the process with your client, build on what you have already been made aware of and see where it goes. I cannot stress enough the importance of using this iterative process of taking each new piece of information and 'feeling into it' to gain your desired results.

For the purposes of this exercise, it transpired that 'Dad' was a set builder in a TV studio. Now you've seen how you can build a whole reading from just one piece of evidence.

On my table, I deliberately put 'REASON' in capital letters. This is because certain establishments are now teaching that you should not give a REASON for a spirit communicator coming through to clients' loved ones. Such establishments state that this is because you are not a trained therapist or a counsellor. I also know that some of them are running scared of litigation. Some poorly trained mediums have been known to tell clients what they must do with their lives, saying the information has come from Spirit.

The reality is clients will often have something going on and that is exactly why they have come to see you, so they can find out what their loved ones have to say about it.

I remember reading for one lady who wholeheartedly agreed with my evidence. However, when we reached the point of delivering the message, her father in spirit spoke about his daughter moving back to her hometown, a place she had not resided in for over 30 years.

Whilst he did not tell her what she should do, his REASON for coming through was to ask her to remember why she had left the town in the first place."

I asked my client whether it was important that her father had chosen this subject to speak about and she nearly fell off her chair. She said, "The REASON I came here today is because I wanted my father to give me some guidance."

Remember this! You cannot tell people what to do with their lives, you can only offer the evidence, as I did. This lady's father simply said, "Remember why you left town." Allow your recipient to make an informed choice, knowing their loved ones are watching over them.

Good and bad evidence

We have to remember that as mediums we are the meat in the sandwich. We have brains that constantly attempt to make logical sense out of illogical feelings. Spirit will give you something and it's your job to pass on that piece of evidence as intended. You will notice this about your own life, too. There'll be times when your gut feeling is trying to tell you something from Spirit. At the same time, your brain will be trying to work out the feelings and make sense of it all. Always try and 'feel' the evidence from Spirit, either for yourself or a client.

One-to-one readings can be a little easier, depending on your viewpoint. I say easier because if you are wrong your client will probably tell you. You will feel under more pressure because your client is there for a reason and they'll be expecting results, and fast. Try and take the pressure off yourself as much as possible by employing all of the tactics I have already described, such as creating a sacred space and settling your client. This will settle you, too.

Demonstrations of clairvoyance are in a league of their own and they are not for everybody, but your evidence should be as compelling, if not more so, than with a one-to-one reading because there are so many more people listening.

Collecting Evidence

I once voluntarily took part in a demonstration of clairvoyance at a mind, body and spirit fair. This gave me a rare opportunity to watch other mediums at work.

The gentleman who was on before me pointed to a lady and said:

"Who is the man in spirit with the bad chest?"

Recipient: "My dad."

The medium went on to talk about the lady and everything to do with her life and what was going on around her. He kept saying, "Your dad is telling me this…" At no point did he offer the lady any concrete evidence to prove that it was her father in the room.

I know for a fact that he was using a psychic link to connect with the lady and wasn't receiving the evidence from Spirit at all – because there was no evidence. Even so, she was lapping it up. I am not saying for one second this 'medium' was fraudulent, as the lady accepted what he was saying. However, he was not providing evidence from Spirit about her father's survival.

The law of averages has proved beyond doubt that the vast majority of 'evidence' can be applied to most of us.

Where have you heard this before?

"I have a man from the world of spirit here who links to the name John. There is also a cancer condition around this man and towards the end of his life he lost a lot of weight."

I actually said this at a demonstration of clairvoyance, just to prove a point. I can guarantee that on this night at least 10 hands went up in the air.

Some people are desperate for a message, and rightfully so, and they will try and make anything 'fit'. I am not belittling these people or making fun, it's just something that happens. As a medium, you not only have a responsibility for what you say but you must also ensure you are as accurate as possible. I merely wanted my audience to understand what happens during such events.

I then presented my evidence as such:

"I have a man from Spirit here, I know he passed with cancer."

10 hands in the air.

"He lost a lot of weight because he could not swallow properly, but I do know that his illness was centred around his throat."

Five hands in the air.

"As a result of this, he was fed via a tube."

Two hands in the air.

"He also links very strongly to the name John, either it was his name or a direct blood relative."

One hand in the air.

I have précised what I did actually say for the sake of brevity and was much gentler with those involved. As a medium, without being dictatorial, you have to nail your evidence down and keep control of your audience, or else the whole evening will run away with you because everybody will relate to some of what you have said.

With one-to-one readings, if you are too vague, your client will look at you blankly and you will soon disappear down a rabbit hole.

Spirit taught me a harsh lesson during a church service many years ago. I had two communicators from Spirit for two separate gentlemen in the congregation.

Fourteen points of evidence later, they both still had their hands in the air. I should have had it all sorted far earlier by asking Spirit to give me one thing that would take me to the correct recipient, which eventually happened.

At the end of the evening, I spoke to both gentlemen. It was no surprise to discover that one of them was taking all the points of evidence and loosely linking them to anybody he knew in Spirit. The other gentleman linked it all to one communicator.

I had said the following:

"I can sense there are some Scottish links with this man."

And…

"There are also links to the Navy and a dependence on alcohol…"

I didn't present my evidence accurately enough. In my mind, I knew I was talking about the same person, but I was being too vague.

What I should have said is this:

"I have a man from Spirit and I believe he was Scottish because he is taking me to Scotland's Malt Whisky Trail. I also KNOW there was a drink-related condition, possibly even a dependence on alcohol.

"Whilst there, he is handing me a tot of rum, so I know there were links to the Navy as this is symbolic."

Did you notice that I am now using the words "I know"? When you are confident enough to say, "I know," it means you are working so closely with Spirit that there are no doubts about the evidence you are presenting.

I must stress again that if you are in a public demonstration of clairvoyance and give too much evidence, the whole room will take it on board and you will end up with a melee on your hands.

Conversely, if you provide a whole range of points of evidence to a single recipient and they don't confirm or deny anything, confusion will also reign.

Top Tip #6: Keep It Simple Stupid (KISS) is the best acronym you will ever use in your mediumship.

One-to-one readings are different again because, as you're only dealing with one person, your evidence will either be right or wrong.

Common denominators

If you are working with Spirit and are standing in front of a group of people, there will be evidence that most people will accept because of the local area and its history or socio-economic background.

For example, you may go to an area where there was a coalmine or dockyard, where a large proportion of people worked. It stands to reason that loved ones connected to those industries might come through from Spirit.

In the past, the cities of Liverpool, Glasgow and Newcastle employed great swathes of men in the shipbuilding industry. Elsewhere, the same went for fishing, steelworks, car manufacturing and farming.

The better your evidence, the better your bond with your recipient.

There are general and specific things that people will accept, but BE CAREFUL. I have given precise information about somebody in an audience and they have denied it. I later found out it was because they were well known in the town and did not want others to know their business, which is silly because Spirit would not make public information that is too personal.

12. 'HEART WALLS'

I like the term *'heart walls'*. It's a phrase that a friend coined when referring to the various blocks that people present. The easy way to understand this theory is that people who have something to hide need to control their emotions quite deliberately.

Imagine you go to see your best friend. She is perfectly well and when you ask her how she is she replies, "Wonderful" and the conversation continues about what you have both been doing since you last saw each other. Essentially, her heart is open.

It has also been scientifically proven that when you are happy and carefree, your heart sends out the largest magnetic resonance in the body. Do you remember the cartoons many years ago that showed a big red heart beating away – boom, boom, boom – to signify love between two of the characters?

Conversely, what do you think happens when somebody is sad? I alluded to it earlier when I spoke about the bottle of champagne. They keep everything in, literally bottled up, and would rather not make conversation. You might even be a little sensitive towards them and ask what is wrong because they do not seem themselves. More often than not, they will deny anything is the matter and will try to steer the conversation elsewhere because they may still be dealing with an issue internally. The internalising of an issue may go on for years before a person is ready/able to deal with it.

The same will most definitely go for your readings. People do not have them because their lives are oh so perfect, they are there for a reason, and you have to remember that you cannot put right years of hurt in a 30-minute session.

Equally, you might be the first person your client has spoken to about their loss (apart from close family members). The fact that they are with you is already a step in the right direction because they want to open up.

Your client will want to know that their loved one is OK in Spirit and they will also need proof of that. If you are their first point of contact, their need is going to be huge and even if you materialised their loved one in the room it would not be enough because grief is about physical loss, too. They could have lost a child, husband, wife, mother, lover or father. What matters is that the passing, for them, has left a huge hole in their life.

One lady came to see me after her lover passed in a car accident. She was having an illicit affair with him and naturally couldn't tell anybody about what had happened. Can you imagine her distress?

I am often asked how long it takes for spirit communicators to 'come through' after their passing. There is no time limit, as it all depends on the relationship between the communicator and your recipient. When I say relationship, I mean the emotional distance between them at the time of the passing.

I was reading for a lady over the telephone when a woman came through from Spirit. There was sufficient evidence for my client to know exactly who I was talking about.

"My word," she said. "That lady was my next door neighbour and she only passed away three days ago."

Conversely, at another mind, body and spirit event, I really struggled to get anything at all for one lady. I knew her husband was present, but I couldn't pull him forward. "He is telling me he needs you to let him go," I explained. "This feels raw and like he passed recently." The lady replied, "I can't let him go, he passed away 42 years ago and it still feels like yesterday."

We know people pass to Spirit, but that doesn't help with the physical loss. Even when people visit their loved ones in a funeral home and see that they have 'gone', it doesn't help them one bit. Accepting a loss is the very first step to healing and removing those heart walls.

'Heart Walls'

A lady who received a message from her husband during a demonstration of clairvoyance booked a private reading with me. At the end of it she burst into tears. It may sound like a stupid question, but I asked her why she was so upset. She replied, "I now know he is not coming home tonight."

13. EXPECTATION MANAGEMENT, SPIRIT INTELLIGENCE AND PSYCHIC AMNESIA

Expectation Management

Expectation management is a term that sums up what I've tried to explain about private consultations. When I first started out as a working medium, I decided the only way I could stretch myself was to perform one-to-one readings. I will be the first to admit that I have never been the best at everything I have attempted, but this fact has never stopped me from giving it my all and trying my best. My mediumship is no different.

With regards to developing, either within a circle or working from the rostrum, spiritualist churches are excellent places to begin. Personally, I wanted to get down to the nitty-gritty at an early stage. Not to prove I was better than anybody else, but so I could work with my innate precision.

I say all this because if you are working in a one-to-one reading or on the platform, the more holes you leave in your mediumship, the harder you are going to have to work. It is never, ever easy. You may be shown something by Spirit that the recipient won't understand. Ask yourself this question: Are your father's memories of your 21st birthday party the same as your own memories of that event? Did something happen that was an abiding memory for your dad but is a bit of a haze for you?

I overheard a conversation recently between two sisters who were talking about such a birthday. They were discussing the same night and the same incident but they had different memories about what had happened. Spirit will try and stick with what your recipient will understand, but can you see what the potential pitfalls might be?

Spirit might also bring messages for your clients that they might not actually want to hear. A friend once told me that when she visited a medium she only wanted to hear nice things. This made me recount two stories about readings I undertook a few years ago.

The father of one client came through from Spirit. My client immediately said, "Send him away, I do not want him here. He took his own life, put my mother through hell and tore our family apart." I tried to explain that his father would not have taken the decision to end his life lightly, and that he had probably come through to make amends. My client replied, "If you do not send him away, I will walk out."

He then proceeded to ask some rather inane questions about a married woman he was dating. This young man clearly had issues to sort through, but at that time he was too angry.

I had a similar situation with a lady whose father came through. She was justifiably angry because he had abused her as a child, but he had clearly come through to try and sort things out. Again, she did not want him there (rightly so) but her main concerns were who was responsible for scratching her car and whether she would move house and get a new job.

It isn't always that the wrong communicator comes through for a recipient. Sometimes, they simply want everything confirmed down to the last detail.

I said the following whilst working in a UK theatre:

"I have a man here who I know was 'Dad'. He collected scrap metals, which he sold for profit. One of his hobbies was to collect Matchbox die-cast metal toy cars, and he would display them at home in a wall unit."

This was all pretty specific, but not one hand went up. I even pointed to the area of the room where I believed the recipient was seated, but still nothing. I had to just leave it there.

I must explain at this point that I totally understand that some people are too embarrassed to speak up and others may be too emotional, which is a natural human reaction.

At the end of the night, a lady came up and said that she had understood everything I'd said and knew it was her dad. I thanked her for telling me, as it would have bothered me why nobody had come forward when I knew my information was accurate.

The lady's reason for not putting her hand up earlier was that I had not said that her dad's name was Kevin. She then proceeded to ask me what her dad wanted – an hour after I had communicated with him. I was totally drained at this point and explained that her dad had "left the building".

Spirit intelligence

There are many reasons why you might not receive something for a client. Please remember that Spirit knows best and one thing you must never do is try and BS your way through a reading. Be honest and tell your client you have nothing for them.

The most positive validation I have ever had regarding Spirit knowing best happened during a reading for a lady where nothing happened. I tried every trick in the book (pardon the pun), but she said no to everything. After 10-15 minutes, I apologised and said I was sorry that she had wasted a journey. I told her there wouldn't be a charge and would bring the reading to a close. She thanked me for my honesty and left. I stood there totally perplexed wondering what had gone wrong and even if I was still capable of doing this work.

Within a minute, another lady walked into my shop to enquire about my readings. I immediately informed her that she did not need one, as her brother was with me and had said that she was not to blame for him taking his own life. It was all his own doing and choice, and it was time for her to move forward with her life. That was it – a 30-second conversation. The lady replied, "You have no idea how much that was playing on my mind. That message means everything to me, so thank you." She then left my shop, too.

One lady was expecting everything and the other wasn't expecting anything, yet they both received what they actually needed. Had I received anything for the first lady, I wouldn't have even met the second. Trust Spirit.

Spirit intelligence is not something people necessarily think about, but our spirit resides in our physical body and when this shuts down we retain our consciousness.

As I have stated, we are all energy, but here's the thing about spirit intelligence. When we're working for Spirit, whether that's during a one-to-one reading or in a public place, Spirit is listening.

You can ask things, you can tell it things, and you can say what you want even before you begin to work. You can do this by sending out your thoughts or speaking to Spirit out loud. State what your exact requirements are. On many occasions, I have been astounded by some of the work carried out by Spirit and what course a reading has taken.

On one particular occasion a few years ago, I was reading for a lady when her brother, father and mother came through.

This lady was particularly unhappy, as I had failed to bring through the person she actually wanted. When I asked who this was, she replied, "I want my husband here now." I tried, I pushed, I cajoled and I willed Spirit to bring her husband through, all to no avail. In the end, I concluded that there was no point in trying. I was a failure. The lady told me how unhappy she was with the reading. Now there is something. I never promise who will come through and experience has taught me to ensure clients know this prior to a reading.

Spirit always sends the right messenger.

Following this incident, the next client I saw was a young lady. I told her, amongst other things, that I had a man with me from Spirit. He was seated in an armchair in a shed at the bottom of the garden, and he was enjoying some peace and quiet.

After only 10 minutes, the lady said, "Andrew, do not tell me any more. I know you have my grandfather with you and you have proved it's him."

After that, she explained to me that she was my previous client's granddaughter and the man in question was her grandmother's husband, who would not come through for her. I said to her, "Your grandfather says he's having some peace and quiet because he was henpecked."

The lady laughed and said, "That's the way he was in life - my grandmother nagged him to death."

I was stunned, as this proved beyond doubt the notion of spirit intelligence. To this day, I still look back at that seminal moment in my mediumship development. Trust Spirit.

Psychic amnesia

Psychic amnesia, as you have probably guessed, is when recipients can't remember something about the life of their loved one, or even something about their own life, that Spirit has referred to.

This can be for a number of reasons, which can include (but not exclusively):

Embarrassment

They might be in a public venue and not wish to disclose anything to you or the rest of the room. My take on this is that Spirit would not divulge anything to the room that it did not feel was fit for human consumption. Do not force the issue, but ask them to take it away, as they might remember at a later date.

Anxiety

Some people, when put under the spotlight, simply forget the simplest of things. If they genuinely cannot remember, move on with your evidence.

Bloody mindedness

Some people will want to make you earn your corn and even try to embarrass you. I remember telling one lady in a UK theatre that I had her grandmother with me, who went by the name of Norah. I was also able to tell the audience member what her profession was, which was a schoolteacher. She denied both.

This toing and froing went on for a while. I knew I was correct and that my evidence wasn't flaky. Eventually, I said, "Tell me your grandmother has no connection to the name Norah."

The woman replied that Norah was her first name but she went by another one.

"Thank you, now tell me you are not a teacher, never have been and never will be."

"I trained as a teacher but I am currently not working," came the reply.

I was not trying to belittle this lady at all, but where do you go when you have such strong evidence and the recipient denies it?

Lack of knowledge

At the same event, I was chatting to a lady and her daughter when their father/grandfather came through.

Amongst some generalised information, I mentioned that he had to use furniture to balance himself and that this furniture was strategically placed around his home so he could walk between it. I also mentioned that there were some old coins inside a brass box in a chest, and that he was asking about Mavis.

The ladies could not recall anything about the brass box, the coins or Mavis. However, they emailed me about a week later to say they went into the chest and found a brass box with the coins inside, as stated. They'd also discovered that Mavis was a friend from their love one's retirement home, who he would sit and chat to.

You can see that there is no need to beat people over the head with evidence because it gets you nowhere, especially if they genuinely do not know. When Spirit refuses to move on with the evidence because they want to prove a point, ask your recipients to take it away, as it may become clearer at a later date.

14. THE MORAL DILEMMA

On August 25, 2015, the British medium Colin Fry passed away.

His passing generated much debate in the media about mediums, tarot card readers and other such people. The debate centred round the argument about whether mediums provide a service to people or, as one BBC radio presenter put it, *"Prey on the sick and vulnerable whilst profiteering from their misery."*

How different is this from loan sharks or even payday loan companies who lend money to people at extortionate interest rates, thus compounding their financial misery? Banks, prior to 2008, loaned money to people for mortgages when they had no way of repaying them, especially if there was the slightest interest rate rise. Those moves caused a worldwide financial meltdown.

On the other hand, 95% of mediums are not in the business of simply profiteering. However, there will be those who genuinely have a gift but might have had little or no formal training. Others might have attended numerous workshops but then failed to apply what they were taught or develop further.

We mediums need to tread carefully, as there are some people who will feel they cannot function and will seek our guidance for their every move in life. I have been confronted by people who practically want me to tell them when to breathe in and when to breathe out. One lady even asked me to tell her to leave her husband so she could be admonished of any personal responsibility.

Regarding responsibility, this is where we as mediums have a great moral duty. If you have any sort of conscience and you are truly working for Spirit, you will know exactly what I mean.

I've seen people who are in denial about situations in their own lives.

They believe that everything is fine and anything I say must be wrong because it isn't what they WANT to hear.

If a client is depressed, suffering an illness or is not in the right personal place or space, it can be almost impossible to read for them.

My point about the 'so-called' vulnerable and weak people who visit mediums is that there are individuals who may be bipolar (or suffering any number of mental health conditions), suffering from alcoholism or on medication whilst trying to maintain an equilibrium within their state of mind. If you do not hold professional qualifications that allow you to see such people, please be wary. You could be leaving yourself wide open to any manner of situations.

15. HASTA LA PASTA?

'Hasta la pasta?' is a Spanish term meaning *'What about the money?'* or *'Where's the money?'* It's not unlike asking, "Where's my dough?"

I am often asked about the money side of things and at some point you might be offered payment for your services. But money is a touchy subject that people, especially mediums, don't like talking about. However, it is something you need to address. When you buy a car or any tangible item, you are purchasing something *physical*. Such items have a market value, based upon supply and demand. While supply and demand will certainly affect the market as far as mediums are concerned, whether it's a reading or a demonstration of clairvoyance we're delivering, it's not something an independent body can attach a price to. As I have said, readings, by definition, are subjective.

There are organisations out there that you can affiliate with and you can even take courses and gain qualifications that will prove you have certain mediumistic abilities, but every single reading is different, every church service is different and you will have amazing performances and not so amazing performances – just like you would with anybody in any given profession.

If you give readings away, you will have a queue around the block. Equally, if you then decide to charge you will see people disappear – as those who refuse to pay anything will seek out other mediums who give away their services. A £75 reading is a bargain for one person and daylight robbery for somebody else. I once told a friend she should charge more for her readings. She said she couldn't because a lady around the corner was already charging half her rate.

The most important thing is to see what the local market is like and think about what worth you put on your own time. If the going rate is £75 for a reading and you charge £30, people will think you are cheap for two main reasons: either you are not very good or you don't need the money. Both ideas are crazy but this is how the world works.

Somebody I know once paid £800 for a reading from a 'celebrity' medium. She said it was no better or worse than the less expensive readings she'd had. Another 'celebrity' medium told me that clients were paying for access to them because they were 'famous'.

The reality is that your mediumship should come from the heart and you need to possess a love for what you do. Yes, if you wish to charge clients so that you can live, that's fine, but there has to be a balance between making a living and caring about what you do.

If you didn't get paid for your work, would you still want to do it? This can be asked of any profession. If it becomes just about the money then it's time to find something else to do.

CLOSING WORDS

My guide isn't about giving you a complete DIY kit for mediumship, it's about furnishing you with another tool for your toolbox – something to refer to that will complement your practical studies, whether those studies are via a course with me or somebody else. Take the book for what it is: a 'guide' to your development.

No matter what anybody says, mediumistic development is not akin to going to the gym or taking part in a drastic weight-loss programme. You will not speed up your development by taking radical action. Mediumistic development is very closely aligned to your true spiritual development – it's not something you can pay lip service to. Spirit guides the way and will open the doors required to aid your development.

I have tried to think of everything that has happened to me – good, bad or indifferent – within my mediumistic development. I have turned those experiences into teaching points. Use them along with what you learn as you develop your own style. I don't want to see carbon copies of me out there. I want to see you out there doing what you do best your way.

I have created this guide to allow you to begin your own journey TODAY. I want you to take each day as it comes with your development and not see it as a journey that has to be completed within a certain time-frame. The results will come, you simply have to have patience and know that it will happen.

> Remember to always say a prayer and thank Spirit for drawing close and working with you each and every day.

Also, thank Spirit for the joy and comfort you have been able to bring to loved ones.

If you would like further knowledge through meditations or practical exercises for working with spirit, or to see where I will be teaching next, please go to www.theroomnextdoor.co.uk. Or, why not search facebook for the group, *'The room next door'* to meet and mix with like minded people.

Finally, never forget these three little words:

COMMITMENT, COMMITMENT, COMMITMENT.

About the Author

Andrew Dee is a retired British military communications officer of 22 years standing. A married father of two boys, he lives on the Wirral, Merseyside – for now.

Following a spiritual encounter whilst serving his country on active duty in Basra, Iraq, Andrew left the military in 2008 to follow his higher calling.

Today he performs evenings of mediumship, as well as offering one-to-one private consultations with his global clients.

Printed in Great Britain
by Amazon